SWEET TIME
DECORATE YOUR CAKE

AN ADULT COLORING BOOK
STRESS RELIEVING PATTERNS

SMALL BUTTERFLY

Copyright 2017

Printed in The U.S.A.

All right reserved. This Coloring books or any potion thereof many not be reproduced or used in any manner whatsoever without the exoress written permission of the publisher except.

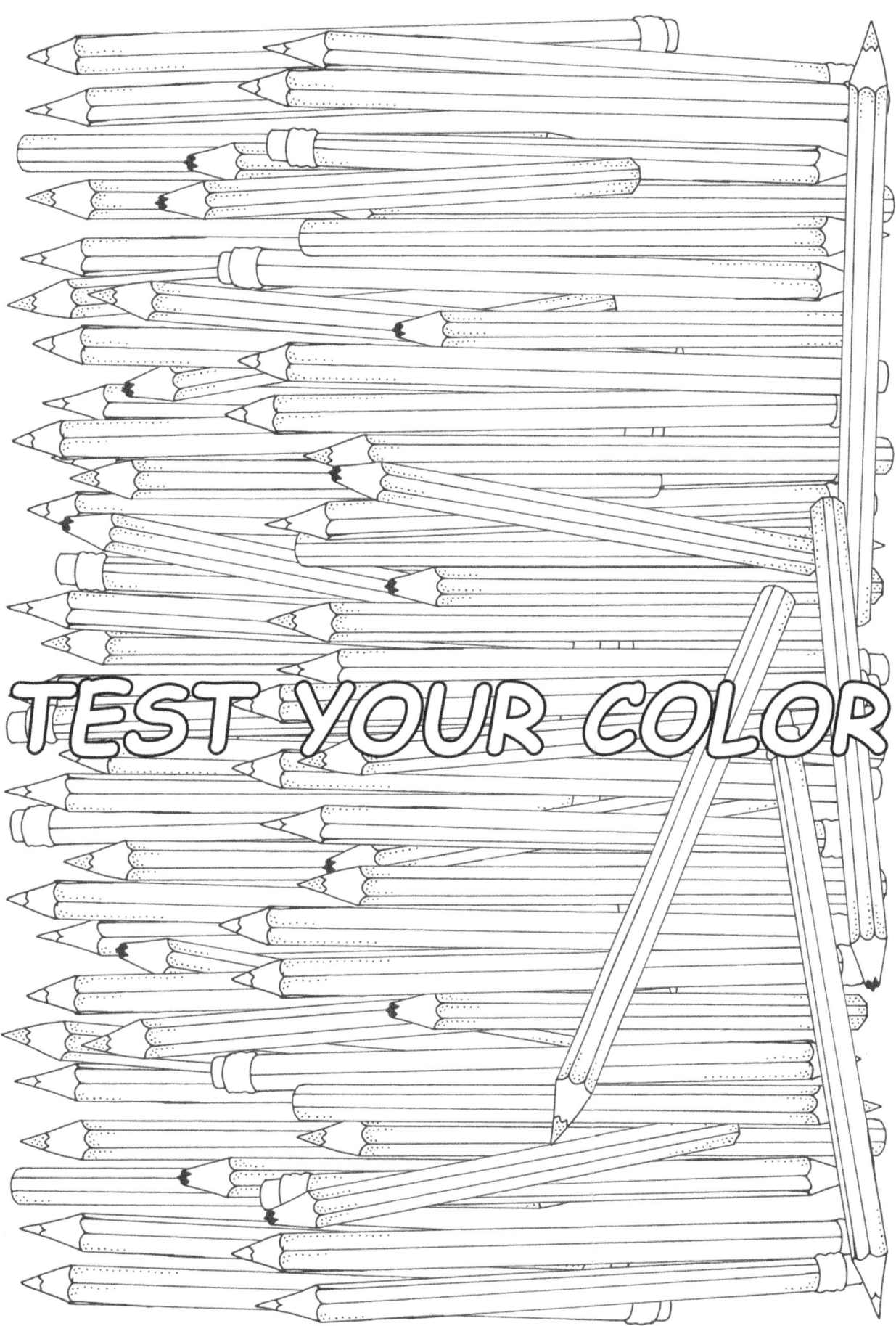

1.

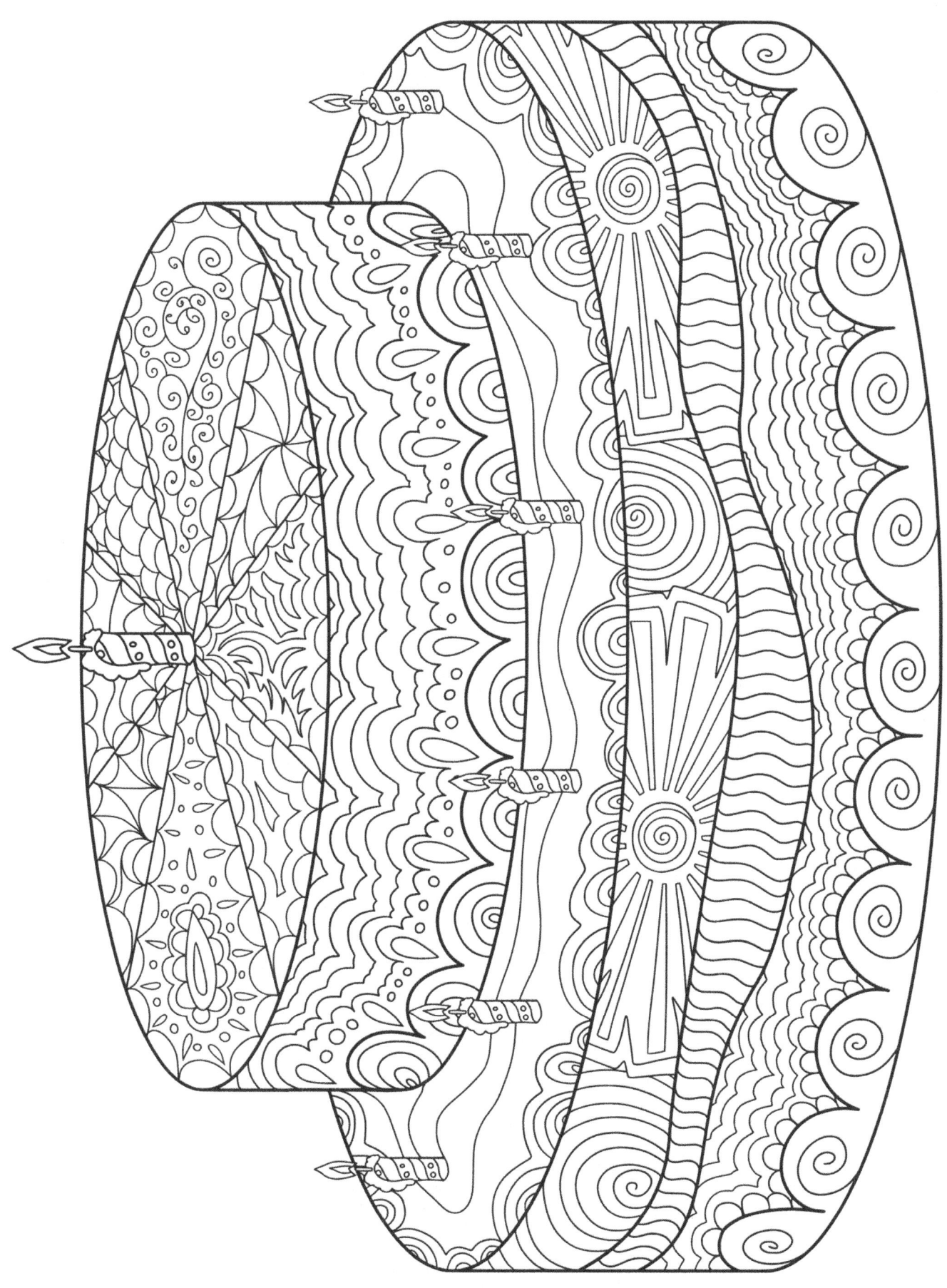

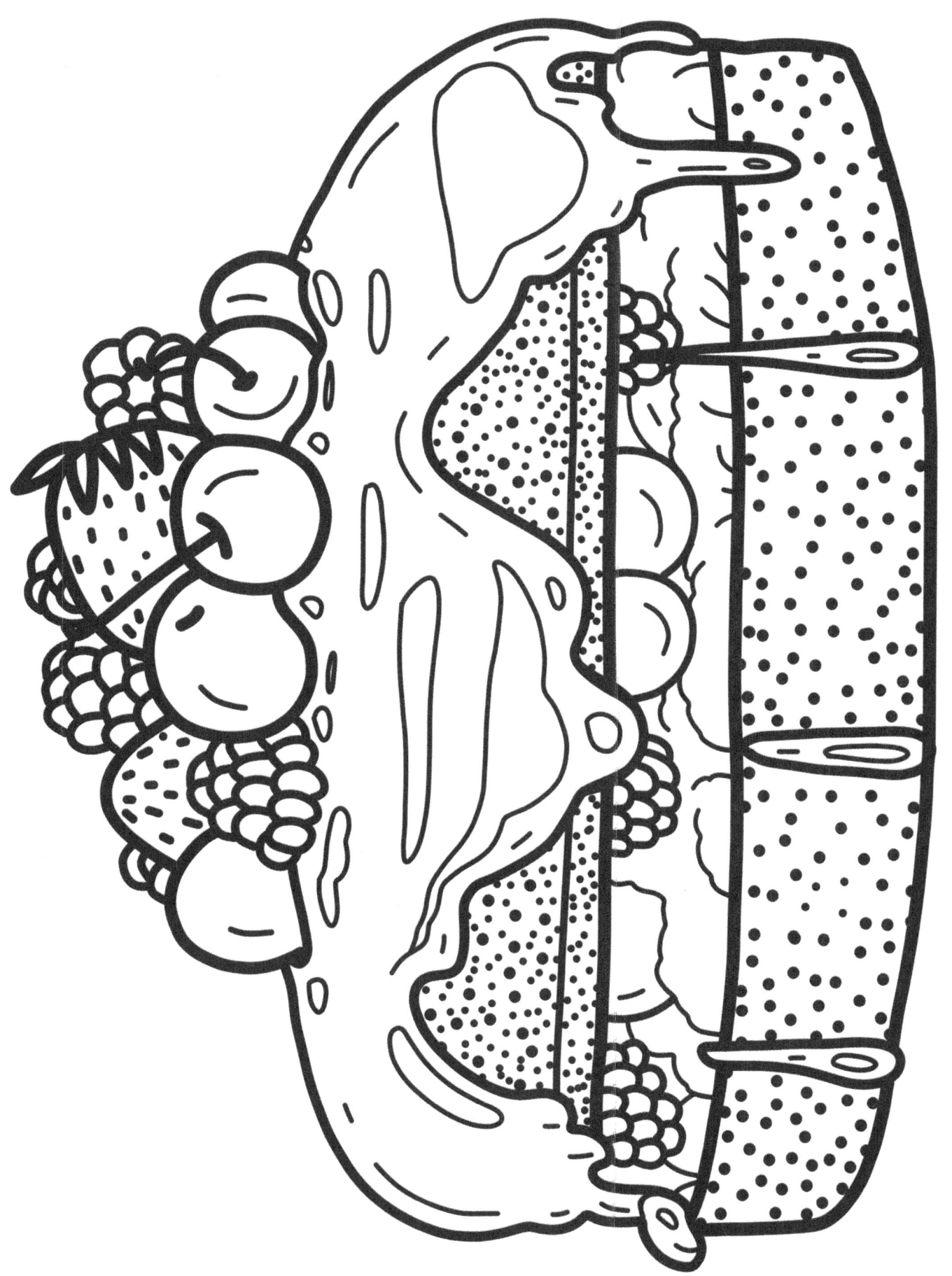

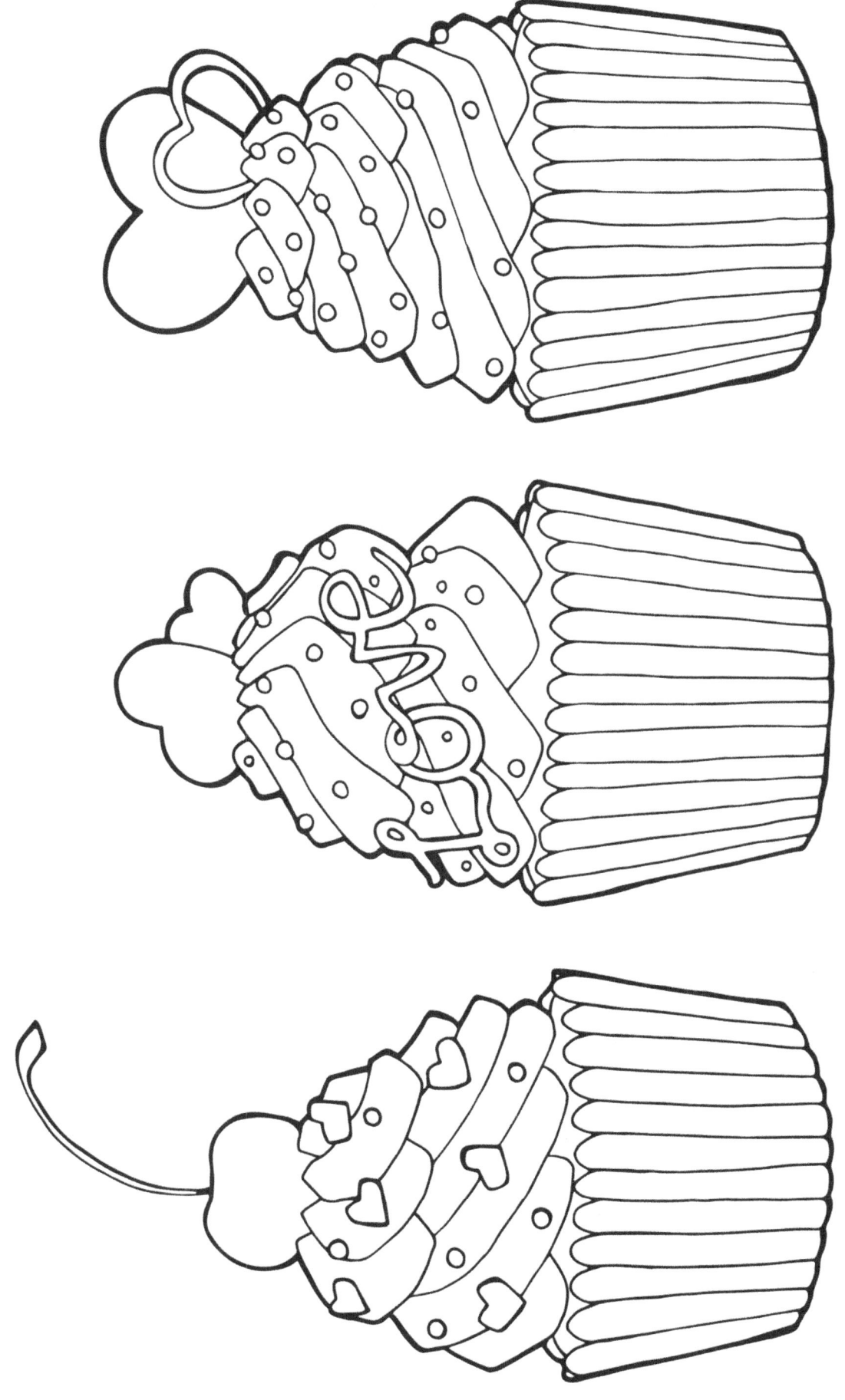

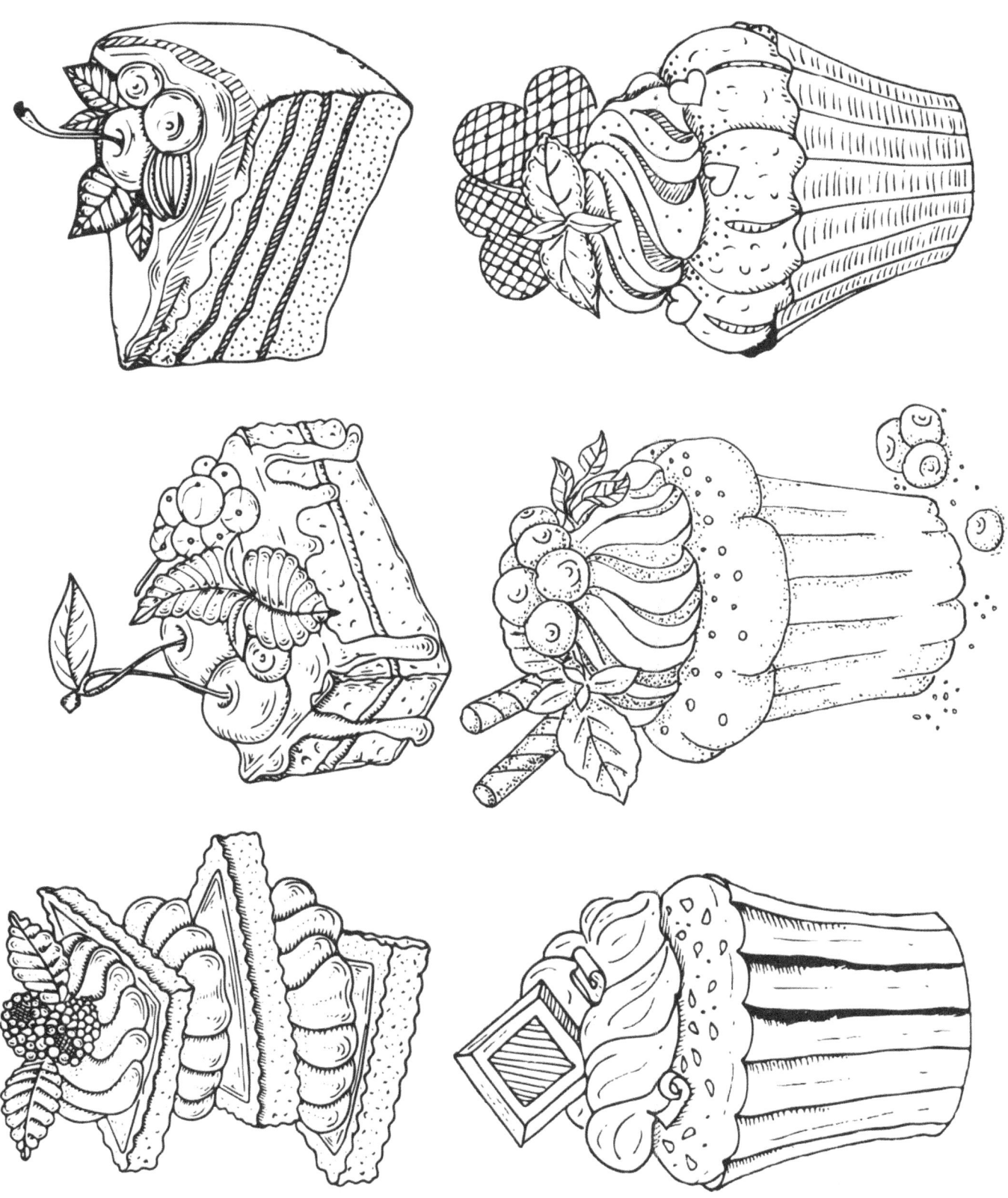

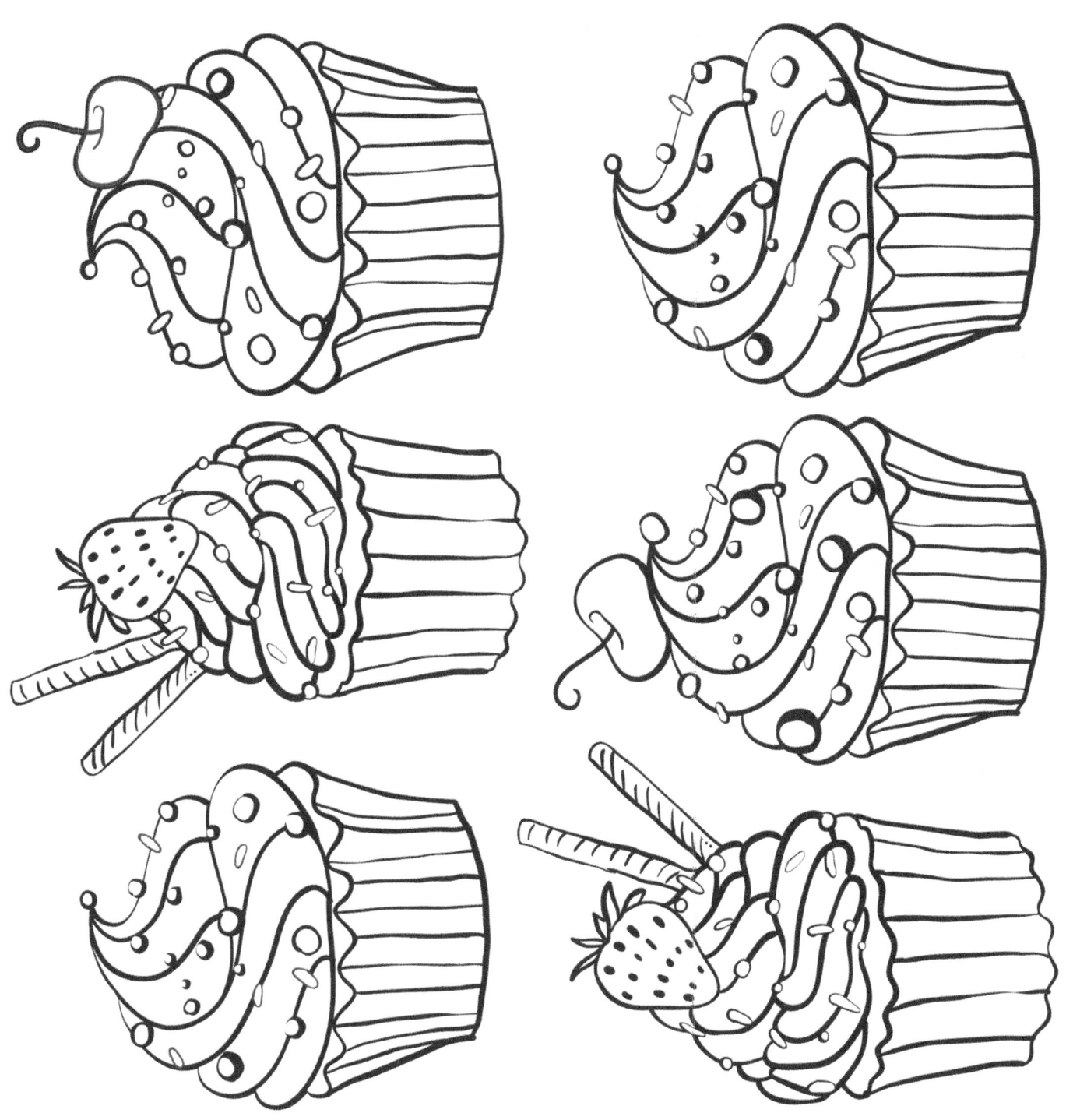

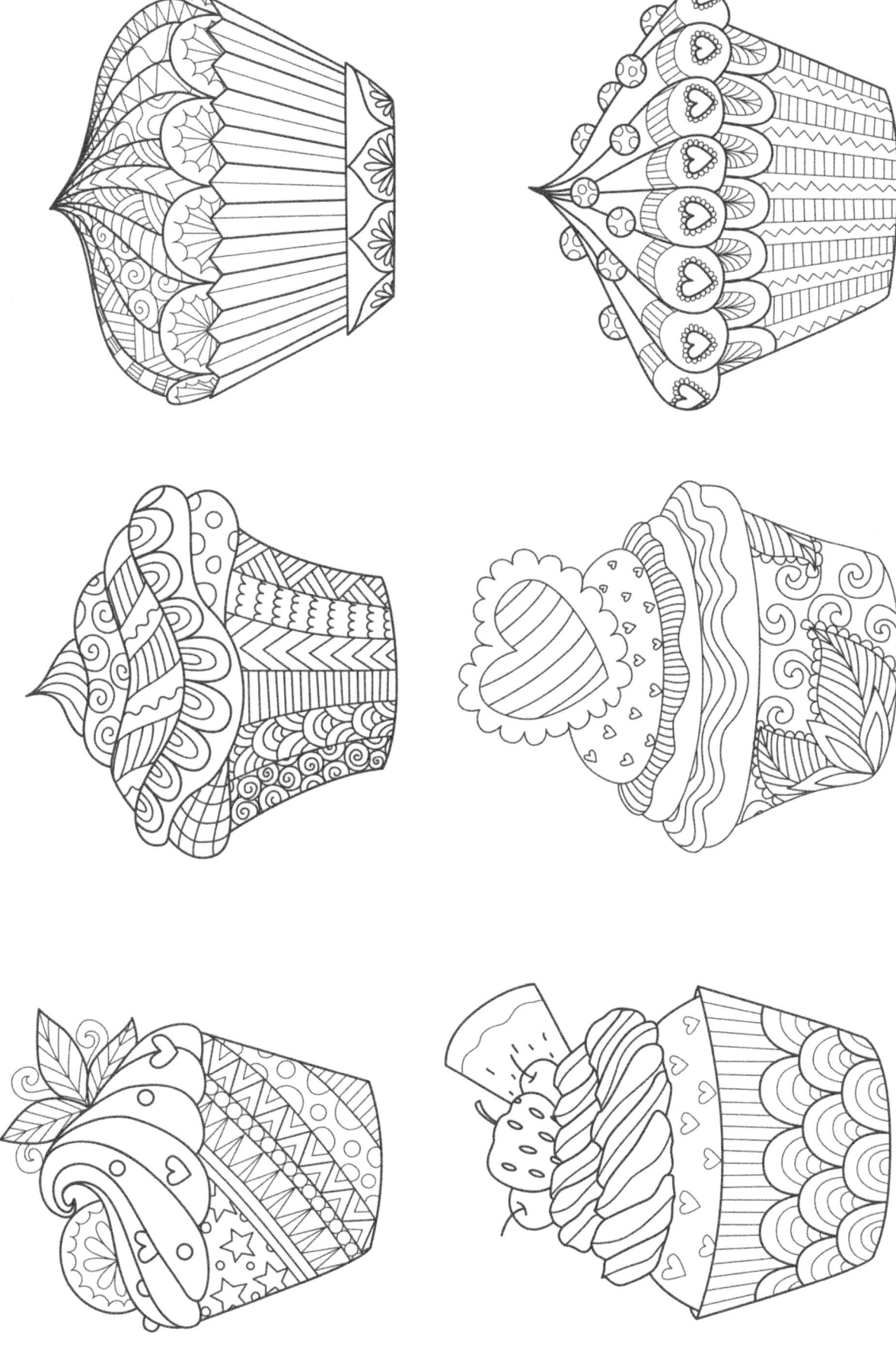

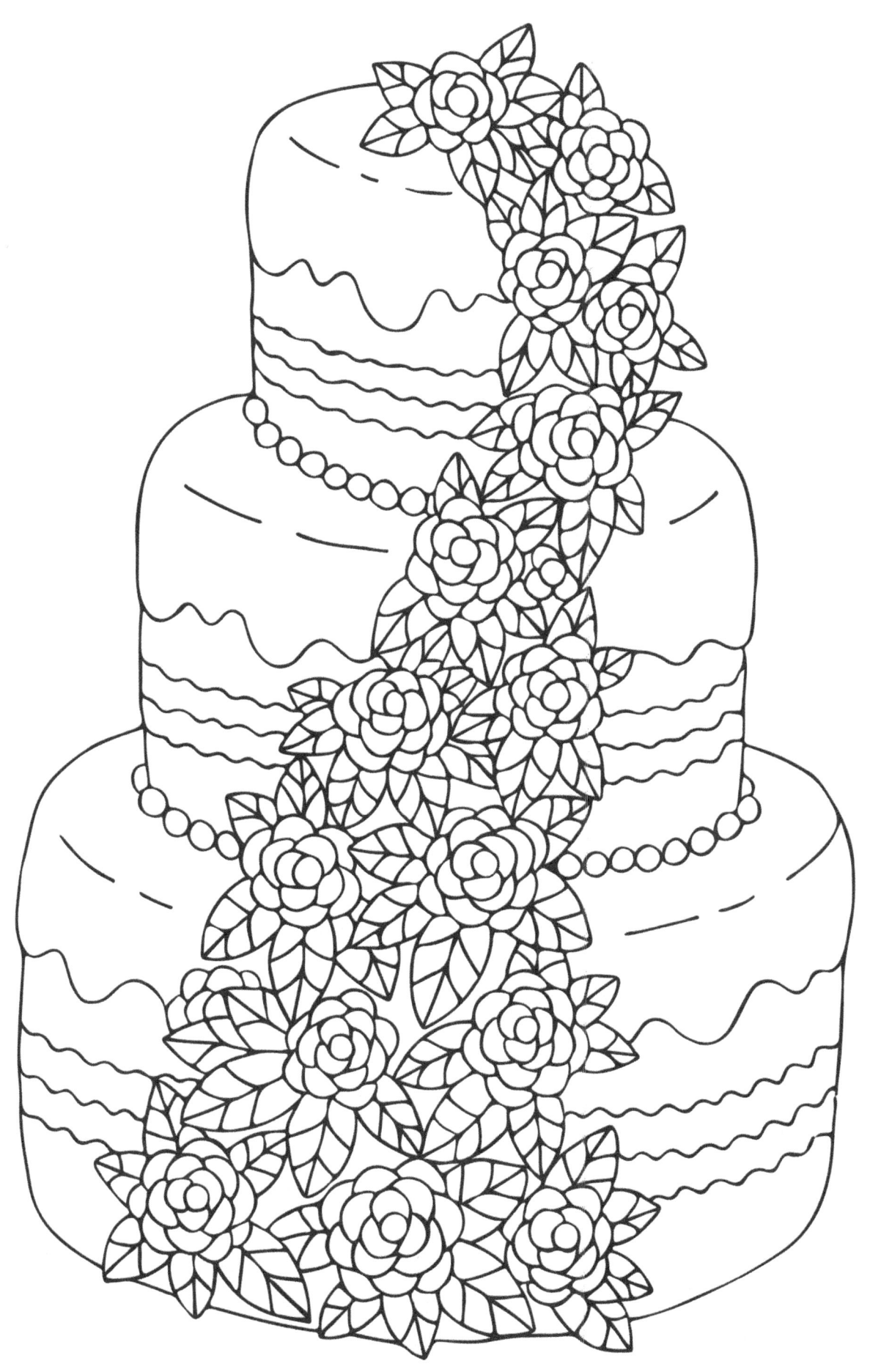

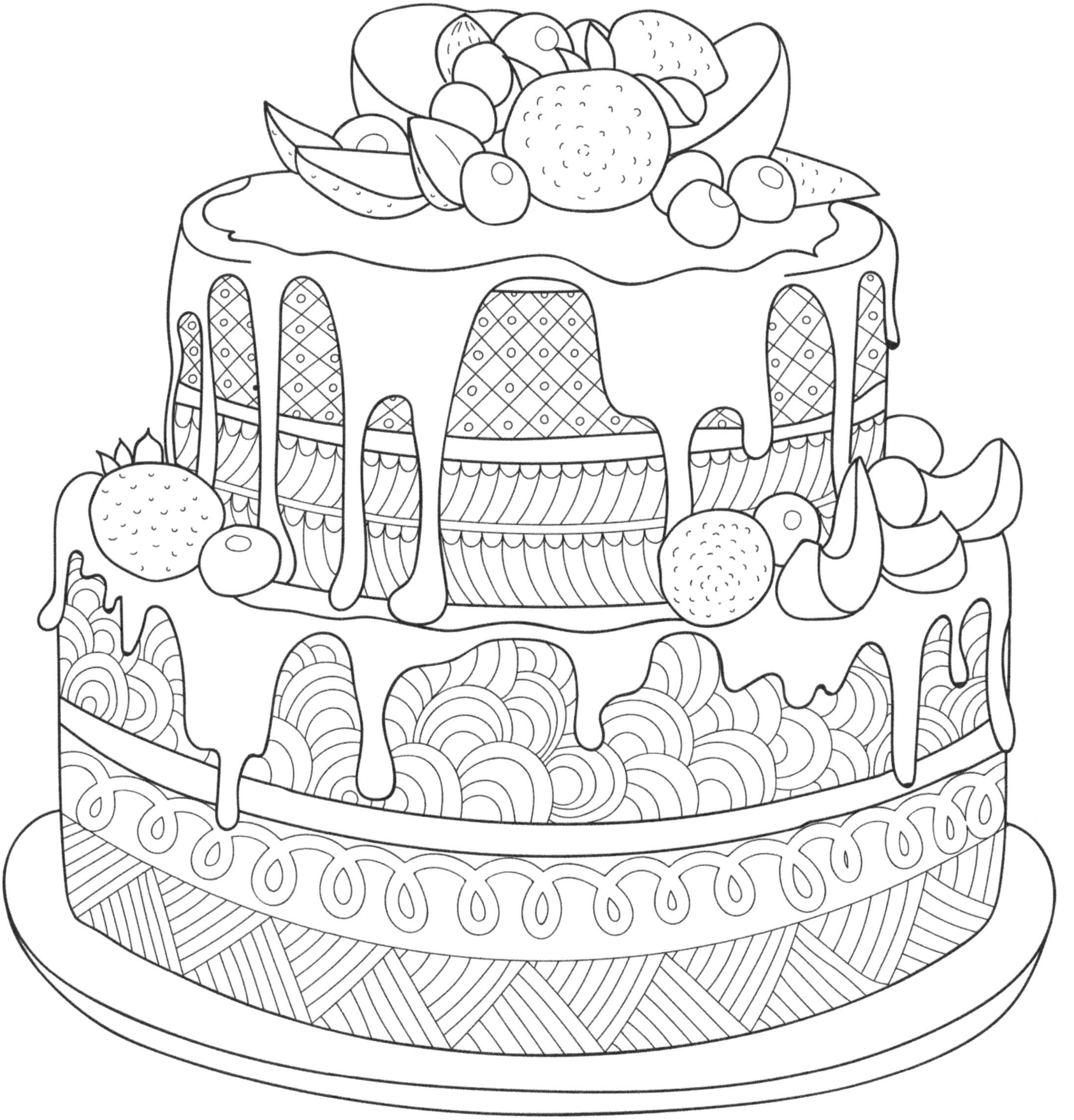

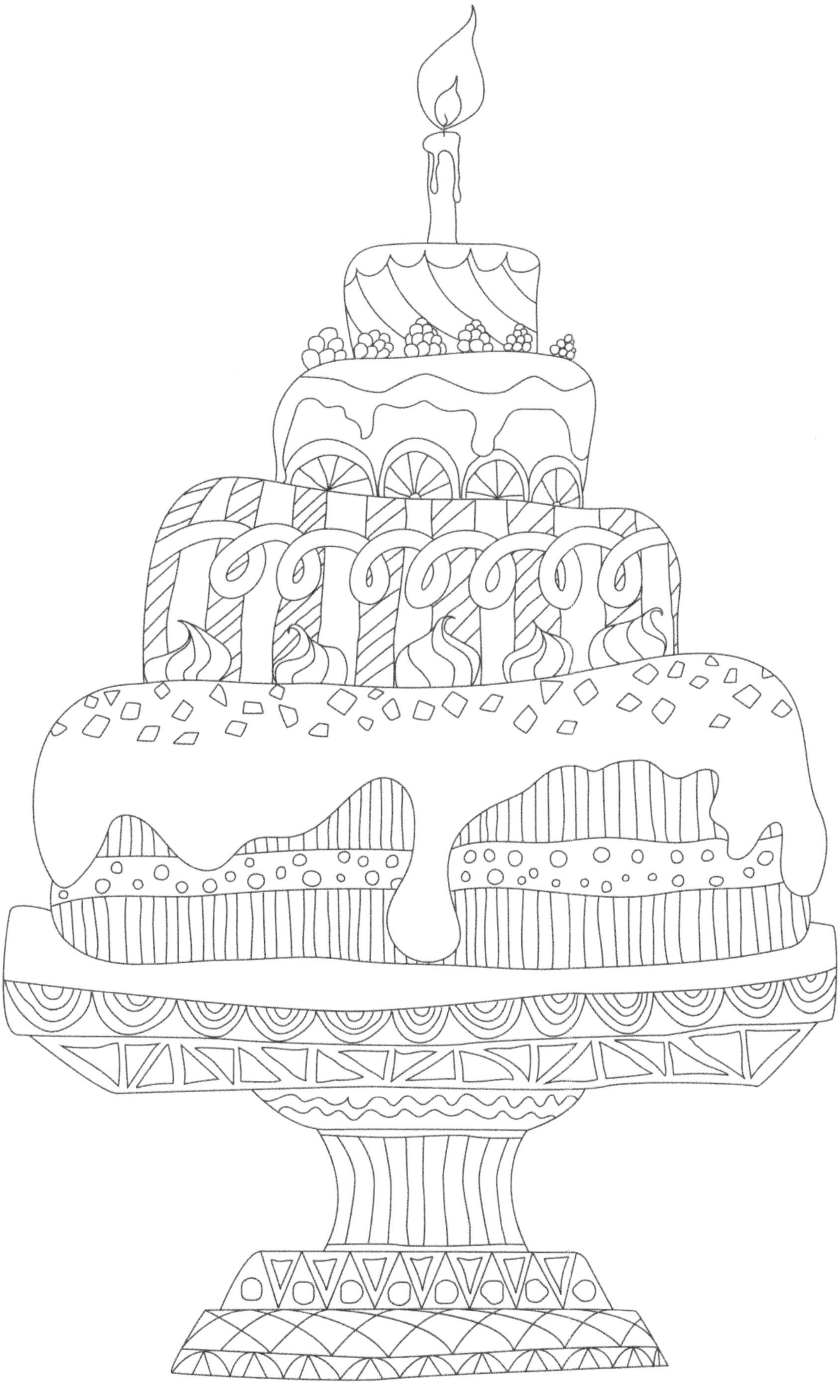

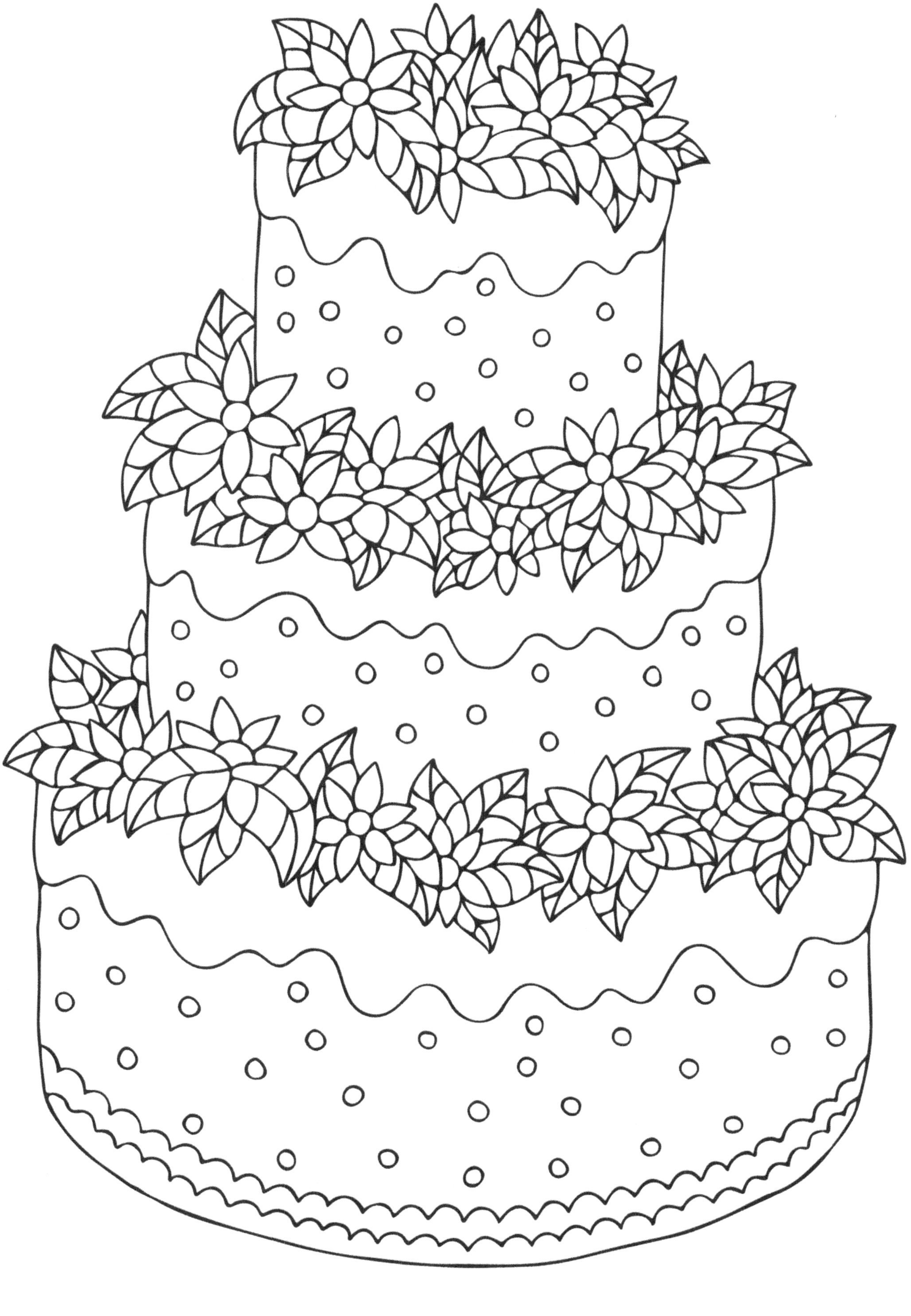

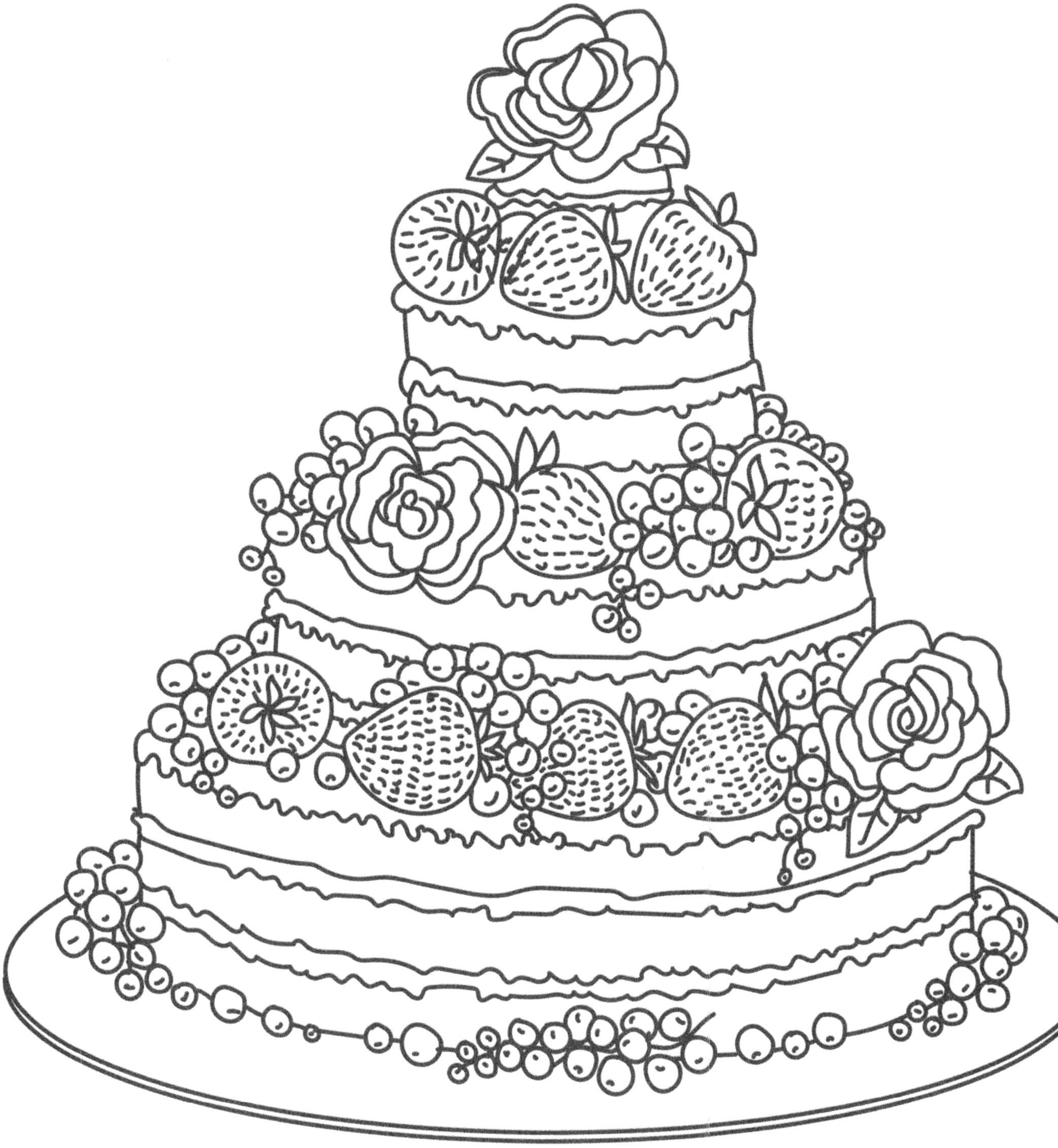

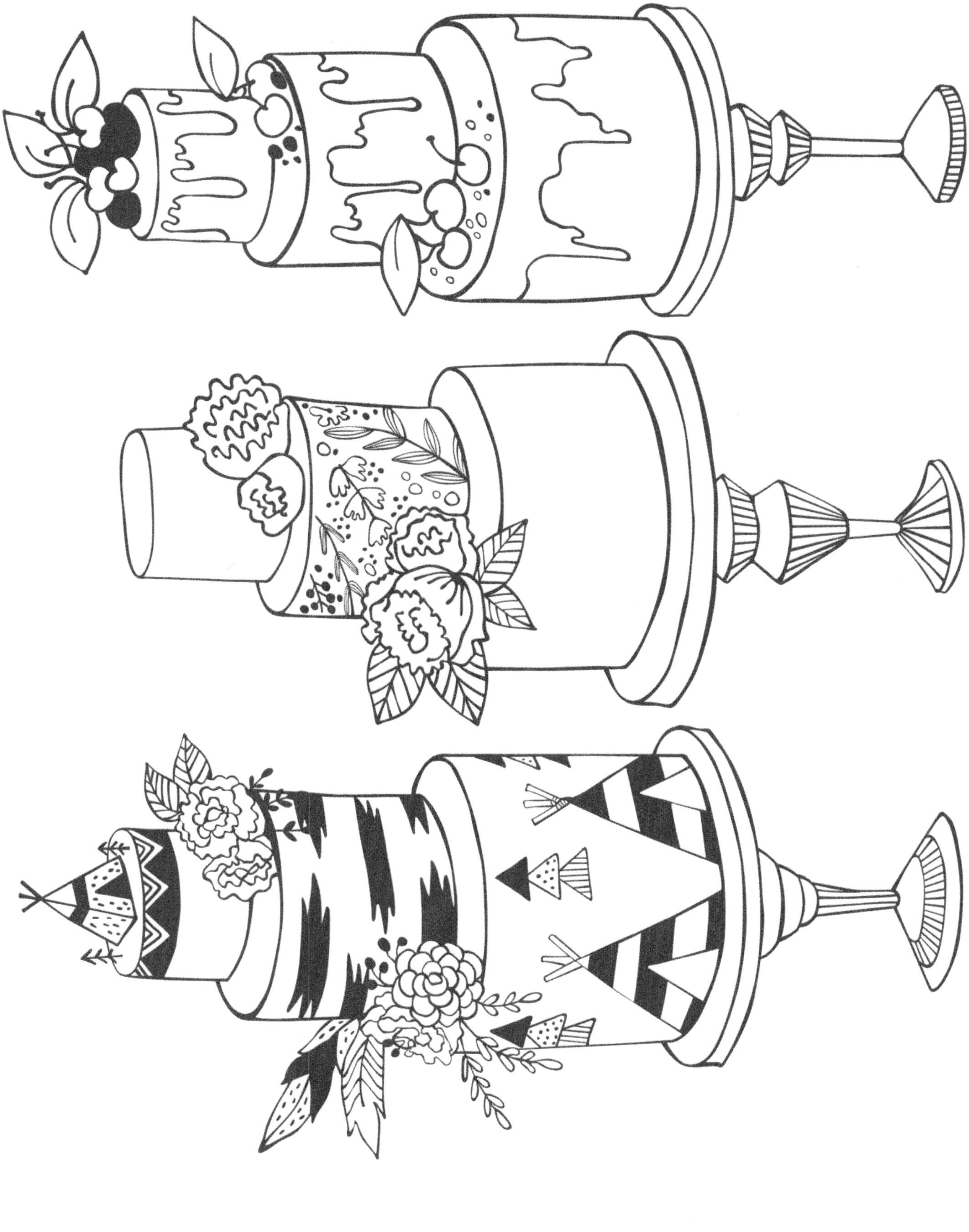

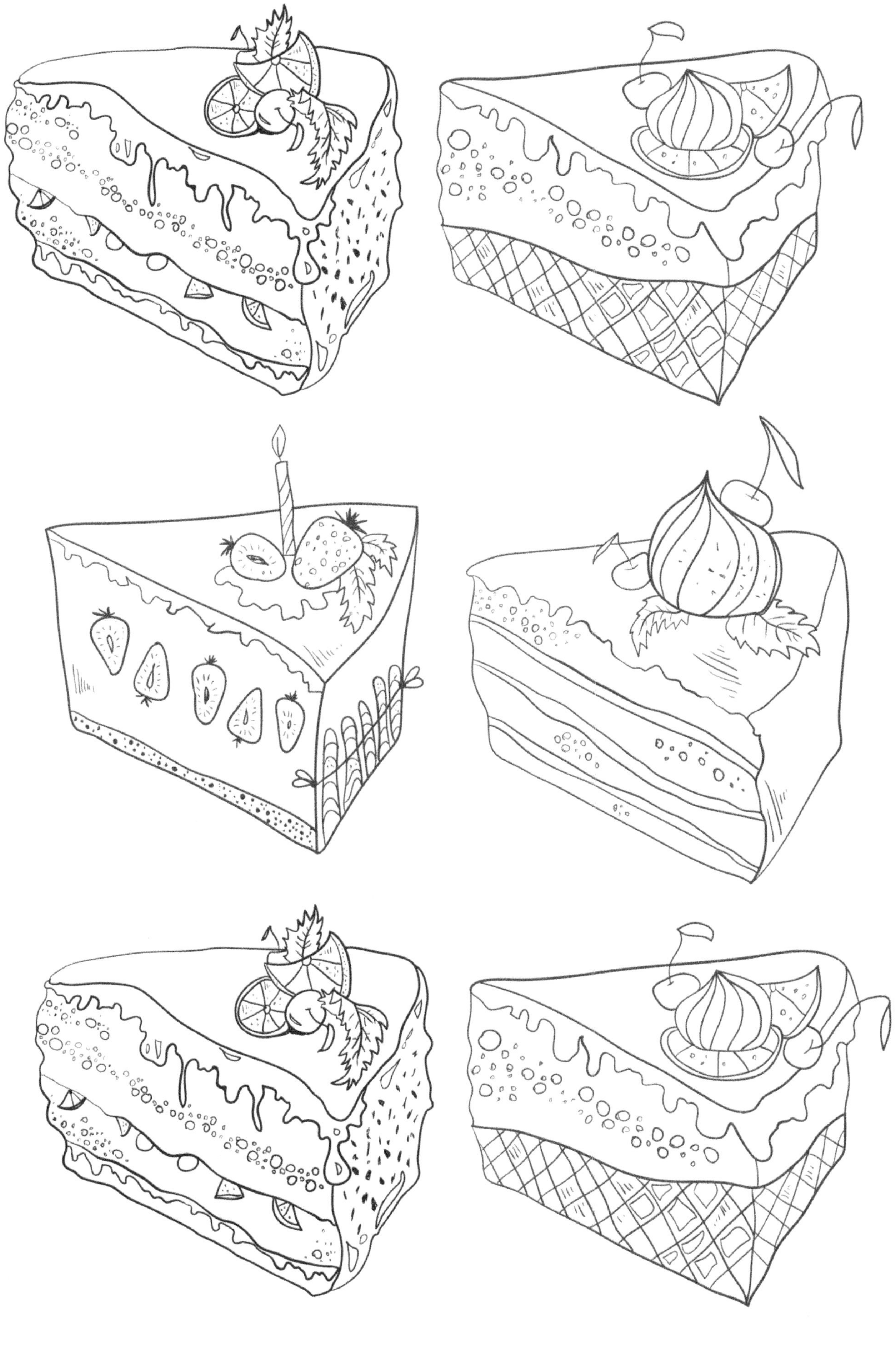

Made in the USA
Coppell, TX
01 March 2025